£4.50
UK only

My Little Pony™

ANNUAL 1993

CONTENTS

Written by Hilda Young
Illustrated by Arkadia

Published in Great Britain by World International Publishing Ltd.,
an Egmont Company, Egmont House, PO Box 111,
Great Ducie Street, Manchester M60 3BL.
Printed in Italy.
ISBN 0-7498-0909-4

A POCKETFUL OF PONIES

"Ring-a-ring-a-roses, a pocketful of ponies!" sang Bluebell and Tulip as they prepared to welcome some very special ponies.

"Here they come now," said Bluebell. "Welcome to Pony Land, Pocket Friends!"

"Thank you!" smiled the ponies.

"Why are your pockets so full of fun?" asked Tulip curiously. "And how do you manage to talk and sing at the same time, Singing Pocket?"

"Come closer and I'll show you!" Singing Pocket smiled. She touched her pocket . . . and out flew some bumble bees!

"They live inside my flower and they talk to each other all the time," explained Singing Pocket. "But their talking sounds like singing to us!"

"We each have something in our pockets," Wriggle Pocket said. "Our pockets are full of fun and surprises. Touch my pocket and see what happens, Bluebell."

"Happy hooves, a wriggling little goldfish!" chuckled Bluebell.

"His name is Wriggle and he wriggles about in my pocket all the time!" Wriggle Pocket smiled. "I hope he doesn't wriggle away one day!"

"Your pocket is *jingling!*" cried Tulip in surprise to Jingle Pocket as she galloped up. "It's shaped like a pig . . . but pigs don't jingle, they grunt!"

"My pocket is a piggy *bank!*" grinned Jingle Pocket as coins jumbled out of her piggy bank pocket. "That's why I jingle as I run about!"

"Would you like something to eat, Hopping Pocket?" asked Bluebell politely, offering her a plate of oatcakes.

"Thank you, they look delicious!" said Hopping Pocket. She touched her pocket and out hopped . . . a little hopping bunny! "May my hopping bunny have a carrot?" she asked with a twinkle in her eye.

How the little ponies laughed!

WRIGGLE POCKET AND THE GREEDY GOLD GOBLIN

"Oh, what a pretty well!" said Wriggle Pocket to Jingle Pocket as they gazed at the Flowery Wishing Well in Flowery Bower. "I must show it to Wriggle!"

"Heavy hooves, do please take care!" advised Baby Lucky who was at the other side of the well, picking a nosegay for the Flower Lady. Wriggle, the little goldfish, wriggled his way out of the Pocket Friend Pony's special pocket.

But it was too late!

As Wriggle Pocket put out her hoof to catch her goldfish, he wriggled up in the air . . . and fell with a splash down the well!

"Wriggle, Wriggle, come back!" called Wriggle Pocket. "Heavy hooves, what can I do? I must get him back!"

"You'll have to go down the well after him, "replied Baby Lucky, looking rather frightened. "No one has ever been down the well before! We've only used it to make wishes, but the wishing magic vanishes if anyone goes *down* the well."

"I'll come with you!" said Jingle Pocket bravely. "We'll go down in the bucket."

"I'd come with you too, if only there were enough room!" said Baby Lucky. He leaned over to peer into the bucket as he spoke and the magic horseshoe on his rump brushed against the side of the well. "The bucket's getting bigger!" he shouted in amazement. "How did that happen?"

The Pocket Friend Ponies looked just as puzzled, but the Flower Lady smiled to herself. She knew about the magic of the little happy-go-lucky pony!

"We can all get into the bucket now!" said Baby Lucky happily. "Will you please let the bucket down to the bottom of the well, Flower Lady?"

She nodded and added, "Here, put this small bag of soot into your saddle bag, Baby Lucky. Sootifingers the fairy sweep gave it to me for my garden. But perhaps *you* might find it useful!"

"I wonder what she meant by that?" murmured Baby Lucky to his pony friends.

"We don't know!" they cried together.

"Look, we're almost at the bottom and there's a river . . . a rainbow river!" called Baby Lucky excitedly. "We can travel along it in our bucket!"

"Not unless you answer my riddle and pay my toll!" shouted a cross little voice.

A little pixie tollkeeper came out of his house at the bend in the river. "You must give me two silver pennies to travel down the river and one for your bucket!"

"Jingle, jangle, jingle, that's easy!" laughed Jingle Pocket. She tipped three coins from her pocket piggy bank and handed them to the pixie.

"Come on, let's hurry, I can see Wriggle swimming just ahead of us!" cried Wriggle Pocket.

"Not so fast, little ponies. First, you must answer my riddle!" insisted the pixie tollkeeper. "Listen carefully:

I have a bed but do not sleep.
I have a mouth but do not eat!
What can I be?"

The little ponies looked at

each other. The Pocket Friends thought and thought . . .

Just then, Baby Lucky started to laugh. "There's your answer!" he said, pointing his hoof at the shining rainbow water. "You're a river!"

"Quite correct, sail on!" chuckled the pixie, waving them goodbye.

"Pick a bulrush oar to help you sail along faster!" urged Wriggle Pocket, straining her eyes to catch a glimpse of her pet. "Heavy hooves and rushing rivers! The rainbow river's dividing up into streams of different colours. We must make sure we follow the right stream . . . but which one is it?"

"If you are following the little goldfish, you must join the golden stream!" called a rainbow fish. "The Golden Goblin has cast a spell to draw the goldfish towards his castle. He collects all golden things. If he succeeds in capturing your pet, he will turn him into solid gold and add him to his collection!"

The ponies gazed at the fish in horror! What could they do to prevent this terrible thing happening?

Wriggle Pocket and Baby Lucky paddled their oars to enter the golden stream as they all thought hard what to do.

"Look, there's Wriggle and there's the Golden Goblin!" cried Jingle Pocket, pointing her hoof a little way ahead. "Jingle, jangle, he's got a fishing net and he's trying to scoop up poor Wriggle! Row to the bank as quickly as you can!" she begged.

As the bucket boat reached the bank, Wriggle Pocket jumped out.

"That's my goldfish!" she shouted. "How dare you try and catch my dear little pet!"

"He will soon be mine . . . my golden goldfish!" mocked the Golden Goblin, his eyes gleaming.

Suddenly, Baby Lucky had an idea. He opened his saddlebag and pulled out the bag of soot that the Flower Lady had given to him. He poured it into the river.

"You've turned my beautiful golden river sooty black!" snarled the Golden Goblin. "And just look at the goldfish. He's as black as . . . soot! I don't want him now!"

"I do, even if he *is* a sooty goldfish now!" said Wriggle Pocket, seizing the fishing net which the Golden Goblin had thrown down in disgust, before rushing into his castle and banging the door really hard in a fit of temper!

The little ponies looked at Wriggle as he wriggled about in the net which Wriggle Pocket held.

"I'm sorry!" whispered the little fish sadly.

"Please don't cry, I love you no matter what you look like!" smiled the Pocket Friend Pony.

"We all do!" agreed the other little ponies.

"You are all kind, good little ponies!" said a soft voice.

There stood Rilla, the river sprite. She looked like a shimmering rainbow and in her hand she carried a magical rainbow wand. She waved her wand over the net and sang softly:

"Soft rainbow waterfall,
Wash the soot away from all.
Golden sunshine weave a spell,
Return them to the
Wishing Well!
Little ponies and bright
goldfish too,
A quick and safe journey
home for you!"

"Radiant rainbows, we're being whirled about in a rainbow whirl!" giggled Baby Lucky. "It's like being on a merry-go-round. Cling tightly to the net, Wriggle Pocket. We don't want to lose Wriggle again!"

"I've got him safely here!" promised Wriggle Pocket. "Precious pockets, we're back in Flowery Bower sitting in the bucket at the top of the Flowery Wishing Well!"

"Welcome back!" chuckled the Flower Lady. "I see Wriggle is none the worse for his fall down the well!"

"He's covered in soot . . ." began Wriggle Pocket, rather sadly. Then she stopped and stared. Wriggle was as golden as ever!

"The river sprite's magic worked!" she shouted happily. "Wriggle's as golden as . . ."

"A goldfish!" giggled Baby Lucky. "But you really must stop wriggling, Wriggle. Wriggle Pocket's pocket is the safest place for you!" he insisted firmly.

"Yes, it is!" agreed Wriggle Pocket, putting her little pet safely away into her pocket.

But Wriggle will soon wriggle out again, I'm sure, and goodness knows what will happen then!

HIGHDAYS AND HOLIDAYS IN PONY LAND

SPRING

Throughout the year in Pony Land, the little ponies enjoy many special days with their friends.

MARCH

In March, the March Hare invites the ponies to his mad March tea-party.

They have lots of fun riding up his helter skelter and eating their food under the table. He gives them all a present, sometimes nice, sometimes a surprise!

In March, the ponies all search for Liam the Leprechaun's lucky four-leafed clover which grants wishes on Magic Clover Day.

APRIL

All the ponies play jokes on each other on April Fun Day and whenever Easter falls in April, Egbert and the Easter Sprite hide coloured eggs all over Pony Land for the baby ponies to find.

MAY

In May, Pony Bride of May comes to open the May Day celebrations. All the ponies dance around the maypole and the May Pony hands out pieces of her delicious cake to everyone.

GINGERBREAD'S PUZZLING CAKE

Gingerbread has made a lovely cake from all the ingredients on this page, but the little vowels have all run away. Can you put them back so that the jars and baskets read correctly?

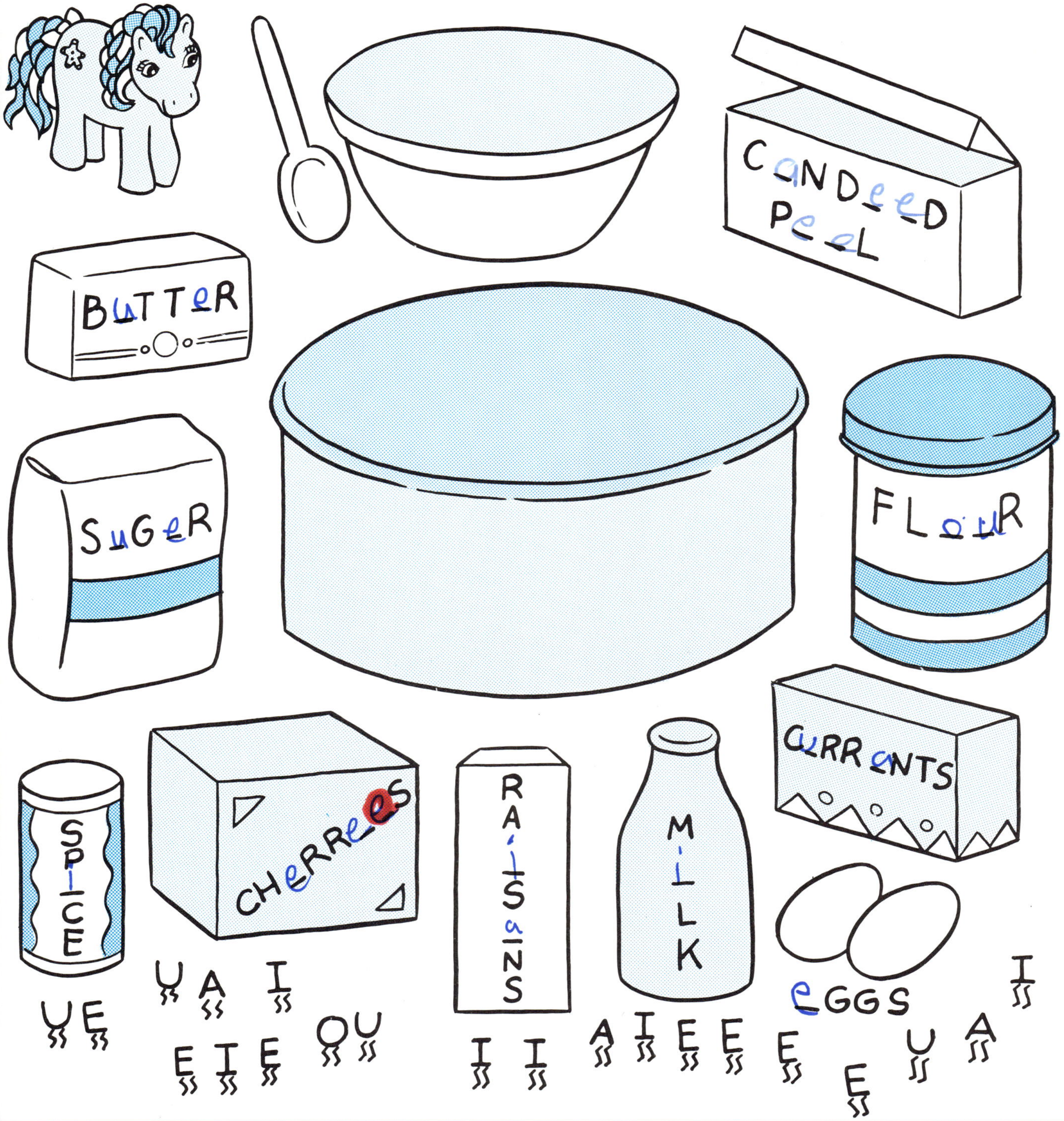

ANSWERS

Sugar, butter, flour, raisins, cherries, milk, currants, candied peel, eggs and spice.

LOVE TOKEN AND THE SHY SPRITE

"I love Valentine's Day!" said Love-in-a-Mist happily. "It's such a loving day!" "And a busy one for us!" laughed Love Token.

But Love Letter was quite the busiest of all the Romance Ponies. Everyone wanted her to draw a Valentine card for them.

They would queue up all day until their turn came. "Please will you write a letter for my love?" they would ask.

At last only one little sprite was left. "Please make me a Valentine for Sweetcream," he said. "An invitation to the parade!"

"I'm sorry, Fudge!" said Love Letter. "I've no more paper left. Can't you ask Sweetcream to the Valentine Parade yourself?"

Fudge blushed and smiled a little smile. "I can't do that," he explained. "I'm much too shy! Oh, what shall I do?"

"I have an idea," beamed Love Token. She went to her tree cupboard and brought out a pretty box and a little bag.

They set off for Candy Mountain. "Why is Love Token taking Fudge up there?" asked Love-in-a-Mist. Love Story smiled.

"Why are we picking sweets?" asked Fudge, looking puzzled. "The other sprites will give Sweetcream lots of sweets!"

"Not like these!" said Love Token. "You pick some to put in this bag and I'll put some in the box! Hurry, don't waste time!"

"I think we will have a visitor soon," smiled Love Token. "Pick the best sweets you can see from these bushes, Fudge!"

"Give me your bag and you take my box!" said Love Token. "Give it to Sweetcream. Here she comes now! Good luck!"

"The lovebirds said you wanted to see me," began Sweetcream. "We have a gift for you!" said Love Token and Fudge.

Sweetcream gasped in delight. "Spell out your reply!" said Love Token as both the little sprites blushed rosy red.

Sweetcream and Fudge headed the Valentine Parade. "We Romance Ponies bring love to Pony Land," sang Love Story.

SPIKE AND THE NAUGHTY JUMPING JACKS

A Paws and Claws Club story

Spike sat in the Meeting Room at Grumbleweed Grange where the Paws and Claws Club met regularly. He sighed.

"Something's wrong! This is the first time *no one* has turned up for a meeting. Where is everyone? It's very strange!"

Spike sat in silence for a while. "I'll go out and look for them!" he said at last. "They must be somewhere!"

So he set off through Greeny Grove, looking all about him. Suddenly, he spied a silver trail!

"Solomon Snail must be near," he said to himself. "Yes, there he is!" And he called out to Solomon.

"Hush, come over here," whispered Solomon. "I don't want you to be caught by that horrid Jumping Jax and all his Jacks, too. Look, there they are, jumping around all the Club Members. Snowball and Twinkles look very frightened, don't they?"

Spike nodded. "What can we do?" he whispered. "I know, I'll go and see Sam Skittle and the Wibbly Wobbly Wizard. I'm sure they can help!"

"You run on ahead!" urged Solomon. "You will get there much quicker without me!"

"I'll be back soon!" Spike promised.

He ran and ran and was

quite breathless when he arrived at the Wibbly Wobbly Wizard's house.

"What's wrong, Spike?" asked Sam Skittle who was sitting in the garden with the wizard.

Sam and Wobbly were very cross when they heard about naughty Jumping Jax.

"Wait here!" said the Wizard and he disappeared into his Spell Room.

"What's he doing?" Spike asked Sam.

"Here they come! The Wibbly Wobbly Wizard has made a troupe of Wibbly Wobbly Men!" laughed Sam. "Let's go!"

Sam wibbled and wobbled at the head of the Wobblies. He is a very special skittle who can *never* be knocked over . . . and neither could the wizard's Wibbly Wobblies.

"Oh, Spike, can you help us?" asked Twinkles as they arrived back in Greeny Grove.

"Sam and the Wobblies can!" promised Spike.

Each Wobbly knocked over a Jumping Jack! Of course, the Jumping Jacks sprang back, but the Wobblies knocked

them over again!

Jumping Jax sprang at Sam, but Sam just rocked from side to side.

"Come on, Jacks, we'll never win!" Jax growled. "Spike, what are you doing?"

"I'm watering you with Trickles' watering can!" chuckled Spike. "That will make your springs rusty! Thanks, Wibbly Wobblies, and you too, Sam. Now we can get on with our meeting at last!"

WHO LIVES IN THE RAINBOW NURSERY?

Why, it's the pretty little Baby Rainbow Ponies, of course! The nursery is a cosy little cave near the home of the Rainbow Curl Ponies. They keep a watchful eye on the babies and try to make sure that no harm comes to them.

BABY STARBOW

One night, when the other Baby Rainbow Ponies were asleep, Baby Starbow crept quietly outside and looked up at the bright stars twinkling in the sky. Suddenly, one of the stars shot down towards the cave!

"It's a wishing star!" gasped the baby pony in delight. "I'll make a wish . . . I'll wish for some stars of my very own!"

"We'll be your special stars if you let us sit under your rainbow!" said a cluster of stars as they danced across the sky.

"Radiant rainbows, of course you can!" laughed Baby Starbow.

"And if you wish on us, each star wish will come true!" promised the starry cluster again.

BABY RAINRIBBON

Baby Rainribbon loves making ribbon pictures on the grass. One day it started to rain on her pictures and all her ribbons changed colour!

"They're the colours of the rainbow!" she chuckled.

She blinked her eyes and the ribbons floated up into the sky! "Look, I've made a rainribbon!" she called to her friends. "That's my name for a rainbow and it's *my* name, too!"

BABY SUNRIBBON

One morning, as Baby Sunribbon was filling her bottle from the Rainbow Fountain, she felt someone tugging at her mane.

"Ouch!" said the Baby Rainbow Pony, turning her head to look round. There was a little sunbeam.

"I'm very sorry!" the little sunbeam cried. "I didn't mean to hurt you. I just wanted some pretty hairs from your mane to wear at the Sunshine Party today."

"I'll make you something pretty to wear!" smiled the Rainbow Baby kindly. She shook her mane . . . and the next second, the sunbeam was wearing a beautiful ribbon!

After the party, the sunbeam returned the ribbon. "Thank you very much!" she said. "It's a magic ribbon now!" she explained. "Your own magic sunribbon!"

BABY BRIGHTBOW

One day, Rainbow Storyteller told the Rainbow Babies about a little lost rainbow.

That night, Baby Brightbow decided to go and look for the lost rainbow. She flew to the Land of Clouds and Stars . . . but there was no sign of the missing rainbow!

At last, very tired and very disappointed, she flew back to the Rainbow Nursery.

But as she climbed into her cot, the other Rainbow Babies shouted out happily, "You've found the rainbow and brought it back with you! It's so bright it lights up our cave nursery. Well done, Baby Brightbow!"

Baby Brightbow *was* surprised!

BABY SUNRIBBON AND THE RIBBON ROBBER

"Let's climb our mountain and go and see the Rainbow Curl Ponies!" said Baby Sunribbon one bright day.

Baby Starbow had been watching her stars and Baby Brightbow had been to the Land of Clouds and Stars.

They were both very tired. "I'll come with you!" said Baby Rainribbon. "I'll just float my pictures in the sky!"

"Won't Spike be surprised to see himself in the sky?" chuckled Baby Sunribbon as they climbed up Rainbow Mountain.

"You must be tired!" said Rainbow Rider as they reached the top of the mountain. "Have a rainbow water drink."

"Rainbow Guider is taking my rainbow ribbons to the Rainbow Fairies for their maypole!" said Rainbow Rider.

The baby ponies were excited. "Radiant rainbows, may we go too?" they asked. Rainbow Rider nodded.

"You are both light enough to travel on the rainbow. But you must obey Rainbow Guider." "We promise!" they cried.

Rainbow Rider watched the rainbow float away, and called, "Of the Ribbon Robber, beware! Everyone do take care!"

But her words were lost on the wind and the Rainbow Baby Ponies waved to their friends as they sailed by.

"I think I'll follow them!" cried Baby Brightbow. "I'm wide awake now!" "I'm still tired!" Baby Starbow sighed.

"Are we nearly there?" asked Baby Sunribbon after a while. "I feel rainbow sick!" "Yes, look over there!"

"Something's wrong!" cried Rainbow Guider as they flew nearer. "My compass is red which means danger!"

"The Red Ribbon Robber is up to his old tricks again. He has captured the Rainbow Fairies to roll up more red ribbon!

"As soon as they set foot on his long ribbon road, he seizes them and puts them to work rolling the ribbon!

"Look, Baby Brightbow has landed on the road! Fly away quickly . . . oh, too late! The Ribbon Robber's caught her!"

"Poor Baby Brightbow!" cried Baby Sunribbon. "We must rescue her and the fairies. What shall we do?"

"I'll make it rain. Blink your eyes, Baby Sunribbon!" said Rainbow Guider. As the rain fell, the ribbon road rolled up!

"Make a ribbon picture of the robber. It is quite safe now that the ribbon road has gone!" promised Rainbow Rider.

"How dare you make a picture of me!" shouted the Ribbon Robber, rushing out. "Give me that ribbon at once!"

Baby Rainribbon whispered her magic words and away into the sky flew the Ribbon Robber and his scissors.

"I'll keep him for a very long time!" promised the North Wind. "You'll be able to enjoy your maypole dance now!"

"The rondo is brightly coloured now. The horrid magic is at an end!" smiled the ponies. But something was still wrong . . .

"The Ribbon Robber has turned all our ribbons red," sobbed Rainbow Blue. "Our maypole always has rainbow ribbons."

"*We've* brought you new rainbow ribbons for your maypole!" smiled Rainbow Guider. "Here you are!"

"We're ready to dance, but May Day is almost over," sighed Rainbow Green. "It won't be the same dancing tomorrow!"

"My magic rainbow will light up the sky for you! Watch this!" cried Baby Brightbow, flapping her wings.

"Thank you, Baby Brightbow. We love dancing round our maypole in rainbow light!" laughed the Rainbow Fairies.

When the ponies arrived home at dawn, Baby Starbow was waking up. "I dreamed you met a Ribbon Robber," she said.

COUNT THE RAINBOW COLOURS

Look closely at the colourful picture and then answer the questions, putting your answers in the little boxes.

How many red toadstools can you see? 4

How many orange butterflies can you see? 3

How many yellow sunflowers can you see? 5

How many green grumbleweeds can you see? 4

How many bluebirds can you see? 2

How many indigo shadows can you see? 4

How many *patches* of violets can you see? 3

ANSWERS:

4 toadstools, 3 orange butterflies, 5 yellow sunflowers, 4 green grumbleweeds, 2 bluebirds, 4 indigo shadows, 3 patches of violets.

TEENY WEENY AND SO SWEET!

One day, four new little ponies came to live in Pony Land. They were so teeny and weeny and oh, so sweet, that the other little ponies started to call them the Teeny Weeny Ponies.

LITTLE LULLABYE

"Is Brandy your pet?" the little pink Teeny Weeny Pony asked Lemon Drop. Lemon Drop nodded. "I have lots of favourite toys that I take everywhere with me," the pink pony said. "I love cuddly, soft toys. I always tuck them up safely in bed each night and sing them a lullabye to help them sleep!"

"I sleep in my kennel!" said Brandy quickly.

Lemon Drop and Little Lullabye laughed.

LITTLE RATTLES

One Teeny Weeny Pony is very shy indeed. If anyone speaks to her, she is too shy to answer! She shakes her rattle instead of answering her friends. Each time she shakes her rattle, she also shakes her head! The other little ponies think this is very funny and they ask Little Rattles lots of questions just to see her shake her head when she shakes her rattle.

LITTLE GIGGLES

As Baby Flicker played her flicker sticks game, she saw a Teeny Weeny Pony building with her bricks. "My name is Little Giggles," said the little pony. "Come on, jump over my teeny weeny brick wall!"

"I will!" laughed Baby Flicker, as she stepped carefully on to the teeny weeny stepping stones over the teeny weeny river.

LITTLE HONEY PIE

"Great, guzzling dragons, however do you manage to eat so much food?" asked Spike in amazement, as he watched the pretty little Teeny Weeny Pony eat *another* pie.

"I never get any fatter, no matter how much I eat!" giggled the little pony. "I like eating more than talking! Oh, here comes Gingerbread with another tray of pies. A honey pie, please!" she asked politely.

"Here you are!" smiled Gingerbread. "Majesty says you haven't got a name yet. I think we'll call you Little Honey Pie!"

One morning, the Teeny Weeny Ponies were passing by the Playschool. They peeped through the window and there they saw pictures and writing about some creatures as teeny weeny as themselves. They went inside and learned all about . . .

THE HARVEST MOUSE

The harvest mouse is so tiny that it only weighs about a quarter of an ounce. It makes its home in the cornfield from grass woven into a ball. The house only has a teeny weeny entrance so that the mummy harvest mouse can keep her babies warm and safe from harm.

THE HUMMING-BIRD

Sometimes the humming-birds come from their home in the Shimmering Isles to sing the baby ponies to sleep. The humming-bird is the smallest bird in the world and it flies through the trees like a bright jewel, beating its wings about seventy times a second so that they are just a blur. It is the humming-bird's wings which make the whirling humming sound that gives the bird its name. The humming-bird's nest is only half an inch wide and its two white eggs are just over a quarter of an inch long.

THE SHREW

The teeny weeny Pygmy Shrew is the tiniest of all our British mammals, the animals which are fed by their mother when they are born. It is just over two inches long from head to tail!

The shrew usually takes over an abandoned mouse nest in a hollow tree stump or among the rushes, but it makes the nest cosier by lining it with soft moss and dry grasses.

THE BEE

There is one teeny weeny bee which is only one twelfth of an inch long . . . and this bee does not sting! Even the largest honey-bee is only three quarters of an inch long. All honey-bees can tell the difference between sweet, sour or salty tastes. They fly at speeds of up to twelve miles an hour and when some bees sting, they use 22 different muscles!

To make a pound of honey, bees may have to travel thousands of miles.

THE LADYBIRD

Which insect is the teeny weeny one mentioned in a nursery rhyme? Yes, it's the ladybird! The ladybird is usually bright red or sometimes yellow with black spots or even red, white or yellow spots! Have you seen a ladybird like that?

The familiar black-spotted, red ladybird is a real friend to the gardener, especially one with fruit trees, because ladybirds feed on many pests which ruin crops.

THE ANT

Teeny weeny ants live in colonies, headed by a queen ant. There are many different kinds of ants - black, yellow and red, soldier ants, honey ants, road - building ants, harvesters and workers. Ants like sweet-tasting things like flower nectar and sap.

Some ants are fed and fed until they become 'food storage ants', so that when a worker ant needs food, he pats one of these ants on the head and is rewarded with drops of honeydew!

HIGHDAYS AND HOLIDAYS IN PONY LAND

SUMMER

JUNE

In June, the Jolly Jingles come to perform at the June Jamboree. They sing and dance and tell lots of funny jokes. Sometimes they ask the baby ponies to join them on stage. When they asked Baby Stella, she cried happily, "I'm a star . . . a star at last!"

JULY

The Silver Stream Regatta is held in July. Lots of boats head down the Silver Stream in a Grand Procession. Tug and Samsea, Sailaway, Barnacle, the Waterboatman Beetles and even the Spoonmen in little cups, all have a lovely day.

AUGUST

In August, when the weather is fine, the little ponies go to help Farmer Barleycorn with the harvest. Junk It's special harvest baler lets them choose their own bale shape. The Romance Ponies always choose a heart shape!

A POSTCARD FROM GOODWEATHER

Goodweather has taken Chatterbox, one of the Sweet Talking Ponies, for a holiday on the Tropical Isles. They have sent a postcard back to their friends in Pony Land to show them how much they are enjoying themselves.

Goodweather always makes sure she has good holiday weather by blinking her eyes whenever it rains and whispering 'Good Weather'. . . and the rain stops at once!

Look closely at the postcard and see how many ponies, friends and objects you can see beginning with the letter S.

ANSWERS: Summer Heatwave, Surfing Days, Samsea, Spike, shells, sandcastle, seaweed, sea, surfboards, spade, ship and sail.

PONY LAND COLOURING

Here is a picture of your favourite ponies to colour.

APPLEJACK AND THE APPLE TURNOVERS

"Applejack, look where you're going!" cried Lemon Drop. "You've knocked over a fence! Stop looking backwards!"

"I'm sorry, but I like to look where I've *been!*" giggled Applejack. "Oh, I've knocked over the barred gate."

"I feel hungry! I'll just go and nibble an apple in the orchard." Lemon Drop didn't look very happy.

"Applejack is getting rather naughty!" he sighed as he offered Peachy a warm oatcake. "And she's quite plump, too!"

"Lemon Drop, Baby Apple Delight and his Hoddy Doddy friend are coming this way. They look worried!" cried Brandy.

"Applejack has eaten so many apples she has got stuck in the hedge," said Hoddy. "She was taking a short cut!"

"You are a silly, greedy, little pony!" scolded Lemon Drop as they all ran to the orchard. "We'll have to push you!"

"This hedge is so prickly!" moaned poor Applejack. "Lemon Drop, please don't push so hard! I'm getting all scratched!"

"Well, it's your own fault," replied Lemon Drop. "We'll have to push hard to get you out . . . you're stuck fast!"

Soon, Applejack was free. "I'll go and ask the Herb Fairy to put some soothing ointment on my scratches!" she sighed.

"Good idea!" agreed Peachy. "Come back later," said Lemon Drop. "There will be some apple turnovers for you."

"You shouldn't have said that, she loves apple turnovers!" cried the Apple Hoddy Doddy. "She'll eat them all!"

"No, *these* apple turnovers will make her thin," smiled Lemon Drop. "Won't she be surprised?"

"I've come for my apple turnovers!" Applejack said. "Hey, pixie, what are you doing?" "I'm teaching you to tumble!"

"Tumble and tumble, but don't hurt when you fall! Over and over like a bouncing ball!" laughed the tumbling pixie.

"I don't want to turn over and over!" wailed poor Applejack. "I don't want to be an Applejack turnover! "

The spell lasted all day. It made Applejack so dizzy she couldn't eat even *one* apple turnover! The pixies ate them all!

All that turning over made Applejack quite thin! I think she'll be eating apples again soon, don't you?

THE RAINBOW REVELS GAME

The Colour Sneaks are trying to stop the little ponies reaching the Colour Queen's Palace. Can you help them get there in time for the Rainbow Revels? Throw a six to start. You will need a counter for each player and a dice. If you land on an instruction square, you must do what it says.

39
THROW A THREE TO FINISH
38
37
36
FALL IN PUDDLE - MISS 1 TURN
35
5
6
7
BABY STARBOW WISHES YOU TO 11
8
34
9
MAGIC RAINBOW - HAVE AN EXTRA THROW
33
STOP TO HEAR ROCKIN' BEAT CONCERT - MISS 1 TURN
12
SHELTER FROM RAINCLOUD - MISS 1 TURN
11
10
32
31
MAGIC RAINBOW - HAVE AN EXTRA THROW
26
MAGIC RAINBOW - HAVE AN EXTRA THROW
27
28
WEATHER WITCH FLIES YOU TO 32
29
30

THE WONDERFUL CLOAK OF FEATHERS

A story about the Secret Surprise Ponies

One morning, Sparkler was showing Snowdrop a piece of pink coral that Sailaway had brought for her from the Tropical Isles. Suddenly, they heard a bell ringing.

"I wonder what news Rob Rabbit has today?" said Sparkler. "Here he is now. He looks very pleased with himself. What's your news today, Rob?"

"It's a very special secret," Rob said.

"You shouldn't tell secrets . . . they're secret!" smiled Snowdrop.

"This is a special secret, one I can tell you!" grinned Rob. "The Secret Surprise Ponies have asked to meet you, Sparkler. Their names are Shining Secret, Shimmering Secret, Spangling Secret and Sparkling Secret!"

"Oh, what lovely sparkling names, like mine!" laughed Sparkler. "But why are they called Secret Surprise Ponies?"

"Because each one has a brooch with a very special key. When each pony turns her key, her cape opens to reveal her secret surprise!"

"What is it?" asked Sparkler eagerly.

"A shimmering necklace!" replied Rob. "If you want to meet the Secret Surprise

Ponies, they are just over there on the banks of the Silver Stream!"

"Let's go and see them at once!" urged Sparkler.

"*You* only want to see their sparkling necklaces!" teased Snowdrop, as she galloped after her little pony friend.

"There they are!" called Sparkler. The Silver Stream lay ahead, gleaming through the trees. "But something's wrong. The Secret Surprise Ponies look upset."

Snowdrop nodded. "Why do you all look so sad? What's happened?" she asked.

"I washed my necklace in the Silver Stream and hung it on that bush to dry," sobbed Sparkling Secret. "But while we were playing hide-and-seek someone must have taken it! We've searched and searched, but we can't find it anywhere!"

"Please don't cry," said Sparkler. "We will try to help you find it."

"Oh, thank you," cried Sparkling Secret.

"Here come the Know-All Gnomes! They think they know everything. But they're very

kind if any pony is in trouble. Kib, Kag, have you seen a shining necklace anywhere?"

"Lots of times!" laughed the gnomes. "Queen Sea Horse has one, the Gem Goblins have lots . . . "

"No, a special necklace which belongs to Sparkling Secret!" said Sparkler impatiently.

The Know-All Gnomes grinned at each other and sang:

"Go to Feathery Forest and
there you will see,
Lots and lots of sewing birds
as busy as can be.
Perhaps, just perhaps, there
you'll find a clue,

Feathers and birds . . . now it's all up to you!"

"What do you mean?" asked Shimmering Secret.

But the Know-All Gnomes had disappeared through the trees, laughing.

"I'm sorry, they can be like that sometimes!" apologised Sparkler. "Come on, follow me to Feathery Forest."

"We'll keep on looking here," said Spangling Secret and Shining Secret.

"Hurry up, or we'll lose them!" said Sparkling Secret to Shimmering Secret as the other little ponies galloped away. "What are you doing?"

"I'm tying one end of my sparkling necklace to this tree and I shall wind it up like a ball of string, to make sure we can find our way home!" explained Shimmering Secret who was a very sensible little pony. "Rob Rabbit told us that sometimes the Naughty Nixies change the signposts so that everyone takes the wrong road."

Spangling Secret watched the shimmering ball unwind as she galloped after Snowdrop, Sparkler and Sparkling Secret.

"What's going on?" asked Shimmering Secret, catching up with her friends at the entrance to Feathery Forest.

Snowdrop and Sparkler smiled. They had solved the first part of the puzzle!

"Do you see all those birds flying overhead?" Snowdrop asked. "They are each taking one of their best feathers to the Sewing Birds who live deep in the heart of Feathery Forest. The Sewing Birds are making a cloak for the Humming Bird Princess to keep her warm. It is a lovely patchwork of colours and it has a hint of magic, too! The owl feathers give her wisdom, the eagle feathers give her strength and the hem, made

from the feathers of lovely nightingales, keeps her voice sweet!"

"But what about my missing secret necklace?" asked Sparkling Secret. "What has that to do with the Cloak of Feathers?"

"I don't know yet," admitted Sparkler and they ran on through the forest of feathers. "But we'll soon know the answer! Look, here's the Shimmer Shammer Bird. He must have flown all the way from the Shimmer Shammer Isles to bring his feather. It's one of the prettiest . . . it shimmers and shammers just like your necklace!"

"Are we nearly there?" asked Shimmering Secret. "My sparkling necklace is almost at an end!"

"Yes, look, there are the Sewing Birds with the cloak. It is nearly finished. Sewsew just needs to sew the Shimmer Shammer feather into it."

Suddenly, Sparkler stopped and looked at Snowdrop.

"Mag and Pye!" they cried.

"What are you doing with my sparkling necklace?" Sparkling Secret called crossly to the two magpies who held

the necklace between their beaks.

As they started to speak, it dropped from their beaks and Sparkling Secret caught it, stowing it away safely beneath her cloak.

"I'm sorry, I didn't know it was *your* necklace," said Pye. "We found it on a bush and thought it would be perfect for the cloak!"

"It would be the prettiest cloak ever!" added Mag. "But, of course, if it is your necklace, you must keep it!"

Sparkling Secret did not know what to say. She did not want to give up her lovely necklace, but the magpies

looked so sad. "What shall I do?" she asked Snowdrop, as large tears rolled down the faces of the little magpies.

"*You* need not do anything!" smiled Snowdrop. "My special snowdrop magic will make everything all right!"

The Flower Pony blinked her eyes and whispered a few magic words. Sparkler touched her magic sparkler stone.

The magpies' tears turned into sparkling stones . . . lots of them! They fell to the ground in a sparkling heap.

The Needle Bird's sharp beak made a hole in the middle of each sparkling stone and soon the Sewing Birds had put them in a glittering circle all around the neck of the cloak.

"It's finished at last! And just in time because here comes our princess!" sighed Sewsew.

"What a beautiful feathered cloak, and what a lovely, sparkling collar!" exclaimed Princess Linnet as she put it on. "It's so warm and yet so pretty! Thank you, dear birds, for my lovely gift!"

"Thank *you!*" sang Mag and Pye to Snowdrop and Sparkler.

"And I want to thank you for solving the puzzle and helping me to find my sparkling necklace!" added Sparkling Secret.

"What an adventure!" laughed Shimmering Secret. "And now it's my turn to show you all the way home. We'll just follow my shimmering, sparkling necklace!"

And they did, much to the disappointment of the Naughty Nixies who had changed all the signs! But the little ponies are much too clever to be caught by them, aren't they?

HIGHDAYS AND HOLIDAYS IN PONY LAND

AUTUMN

SEPTEMBER

Each year on Blackberrying Day, the Sweetberry Ponies invite their friends to a Blackberry Breakfast of toast and jam. Then everyone is given a basket to collect the biggest, juiciest berries they can find to make this year's jams, jellies and pies.

"Blackberry Pie certainly makes us work for our breakfast!" laughed Bluebell.

"Tommy Tucker's singing as well!" giggled Daffodil.

OCTOBER

All the little ponies enjoy Masquerade's fancy dress Halloween party. Everyone wears a mask and has great fun ducking for apples and eating Gingerbread's lovely sticky treacle toffee and gingerbread witches. The Weather Witch and Magician Muddle are two special guests.

NOVEMBER

Each year Fizzy grows her very special flowers in a very secret place. She picks them on Fizziwhizz Night and her special safe fizziwhizz magic sets them alight. They whizz and fizz in the night sky all over Pony Land. The baby ponies love to hold their own baby pony sparklers. Best of all, the fizziwhizzes never harm anyone!

A PROBLEM FOR LUCY LADYBIRD

The Petite Ponies were playing hide and seek when along came Lucy Ladybird. "May I play too?" she asked.

"I'll hide in a teacup!" said Lucy to herself. "Lucy's hiding in the teacup!" called Whirly. "I can see her orangey red colour!"

Next time, Lucy hid in the Mane Delights Beauty Shoppe. "I spy a spotted ladybird!" called Topper with a chuckle.

Lucy hid behind a huge tree in front of a puddle. She peeped out and Puddles saw her reflection in the puddle!

"This isn't much fun! The Petite Ponies always find me!" sighed Lucy. "If only I could find a really good hiding place!"

"I know just the place for *you!*" smiled the Flower Lady who had heard Lucy. "Come with me, Lucy, you'll love it!"

"It's a perfect hiding place!" giggled Lucy, as she crept into the middle of the largest flower. "They'll never find me here!"

She was right! In the end, the Flower Lady had to show the ponies where Lucy was. "She's a ladybird flower!" laughed Floater.

DANCE, DANCE, BABY BALLERINA PONIES!

One day, four little Baby Ballerina Ponies were practising their steps.

"Heavy hooves and muddled toes!" sighed one pony. "We'll never get these dance steps right!"

Just then, she had an idea. She tied a ribbon bow *underneath* the heel of one ballet shoe.

"If I don't want to tread on my ribbon bow, I'll have to dance on just one toe!" she sang happily.

"Well done!" cried her Baby Ballerina Pony friends as she prettily pointed her toe. "Well done, Baby Toe Dancer!"

"If I pretend I'm a feather, perhaps I can *move* like a feather!" said another pony. "Yes, I'm dancing, light as a feather, with soft steps. I like that! It shall be my name . . . Baby Soft Steps!"

"I need a name too!" said a

pony, as she danced on her tippy toes in and out of the sunbeams which Mr Sun had allowed to dance across the floor.

"I think I'll call myself . . . "

"Baby Tippy Toes!" chorused her friends, and the sunbeams shone brighter than ever.

"You can all dance daintily now," sobbed poor Baby Sweet Steps. "But I still can't get my steps right!"

"Have a sugared clover-leaf! They taste really delicious!" said her friends, trying to cheer her up.

"Mmm, lovely and sweet! Oh, it's floating away. I must catch it!"

As she danced along trying to catch the clover-leaf, she suddenly realised that she was dancing the right steps at last!

"Sweet steps for a sweet clover, Baby Sweet Steps!" chuckled the clover-leaf.

I think it was a lucky four-leafed clover, don't you?

BEACH BALL TAKES A TRIP!

"There goes Sailaway on another trip," sighed Beach Ball. "I wish I had a boat!" "No problem!" said the Sand Shaper.

"There you are, Beach Ball . . . a ball boat of your very own. Off you go!" "Thank you!" cheered Beach Ball.

"Will you please come with me to the Isle of Balloons?" asked Beach Ball. "I'd like to see the Balloon Man."

"Happy hooves, this is fun!" sang Beach Ball in delight. She trailed her hoof in the water and colourful balls appeared.

"Help!" cried a voice. "The sky sprites have pricked us with their lightning needles. We're losing our shapes!"

"It's the Float Arounds! They've been giving a display for King Neptune. Let's help them!" said the Sand Shaper.

Using his magical brush, the Sand Shaper shaped some large seagulls who flew swiftly up into the sky.

"Float Arounds, float down and land on my beach balls! They will keep you afloat for a while!" called Beach Ball.

"Hurray! The seagulls are chasing away those naughty sky sprites! Well done, Sand Shaper! You *are* clever!"

"I'll soon pump you up again!" promised the Balloon Man as the Float Arounds came floating on to the beach.

Later, the Balloon Man and the Float Arounds put on a special show to thank the Sand Shaper and Beach Ball.

Beach Ball did enjoy her first trip in her ball boat. Where do you think she will go next?

THE FLOWER LADY IS UPSET!

Once,when the Flower Lady was returning from a visit to the Magic Garden to see her friends the Glittering Ponies, she had a horrid shock!

The Nasty Gnomes had waited until she had left and then they had wrecked her garden. They had torn up her fruit bushes and trampled all over her pretty flowers. And they had filled her pretty pool with dirty water!

The Flower Lady sat down on her garden tuffet and started to cry.

"Please don't cry!" cooed Sweet Lily's lovebirds. "We're sure the little ponies will help you to make your garden pretty again. Go indoors and have a rest. Make yourself a pot of honeyade, and leave the rest to us!"

Later, a group of little ponies arrived at Flower Cottage. Posey carried a hoe and a rake, Trickles held her watering can and the Flower Ponies carried trowels, spades and packets of magic wildflower seeds.

The little ponies dug and hoed, planted and sowed. Trickles emptied out the dirty water and filled the pool with fresh water from the Silver Stream.

Bluebell pawed the ground and bunches of pretty bluebells sprang up. Daffodil blew her daffodil trumpet, making bunches of daffodils appear all over the garden.

Tulip planted magic tulip seeds on

either side of the cottage pathway. They sprang up at once, like tall soldiers in smart red uniforms.

Then the Flower Ponies sang softly together:

"Planted seeds in plenty grow,
Flowers spring up as we sow,
Fill the ground with flowers bright!
Make a truly wondrous sight!"

Just at that moment, the Flower Lady came out and saw that her garden was once again filled with glorious colour.

But suddenly she gave a cry of dismay . . . the Naughty Gnomes were peeping at her over the hedge.

Tulip had seen them too and she chuckled to herself as she sang:

"Tulip flowers, turn red soldier smart!
Chase the Naughty Gnomes away!
Let them not return to Pony Land
For one year and a day!"

The red tulips changed into red uniformed soldiers! They jumped up from the flowerbed and started to chase away the Naughty Gnomes, who were very frightened.

"I've never had tulip soldiers in my garden before!" laughed the Flower Lady.

"These are my own special tulip soldiers," said Tulip. "Tomorrow your garden will have them back again as lovely tall flowers, but if danger ever threatens you, just say 'On guard, tulip soldiers!' and they will stop anyone destroying your garden!"

Do you think the Naughty Gnomes will try again?

"Shivering feathers, we should never have come to Pony Land in this snowy weather!" said Lovey Lovebird.

"You poor little birds!" cried Brightglow. "How cold you look! Don't stay in that tree all night."

"Come with me to the hollow oak. You can both sleep there tonight. But it may be a little bit draughty!"

The star fairies and their stars watched as Brightglow made a warm blanket for the birds with her beautiful hair.

"You are kind, Brightglow!" said the stars. "We will stay and make you glow in the dark to help anyone in trouble."

MEET THE ROCKIN' BEAT PONIES

"Sing a song of Pony Land,
The ponies sing and play!
Four Rockin' Beat Ponies
Welcome you today!"

Pretty Beat sang to her little pony audience which crowded the open air stage in Dream Castle Meadows.

"Come on, everyone, I want you to beat your hooves in time to our music!" called Pretty Beat. "One, two, three, four. One, two, three, four!"

It was such a pretty beat that soon the little ponies and even the trees and flowers and blades of grass were swaying in time to the music.

"Heavy hooves, my tune is fading away again halfway through my guitar playing," sighed Half Note.

"Not to worry, you play one half of the tune and we'll play the other half!" Pretty Beat promised.

"*I* can hear any note," laughed Tuneful. "If I wriggle my nose, I can hear the music of whirling butterfly wings or the whispering of trees. I can hear your fading guitar notes too!"

"We'll all play off stage so that Sweet Notes can have the solo singing spot," said Half Note. "Come on, Sweet Notes, take centre stage, the solo spot's all yours!"

Sweet Notes started to sing so sweetly that all the birds in Pony Land joined in too!

"She's got a new backing group!" giggled the other Rockin' Beat Ponies. "Listen to Sweet Notes and the Sweet Birdies!"

WIZARD WANTALL AND THE SNOWDROP CROWN

One day, as Ice Crystal, Snowdrop and Spike were on their way to the Land of Ice and Snow, they heard some voices.

It was Wizard Wantall talking to his helper, Get It. "I want you to get the Crystal Snowdrop Crown!" he demanded.

"Whoever wears the Snowdrop Crown rules the land. Make sure the Snowflake Princess is *not* crowned today, Get It!"

"Let's go to the crowning ceremony!" whispered Spike as Get It argued with the wizard. "We have to stop Get It!"

"We must warn the princess," said Snowdrop. "Here comes Tex! Perhaps he can help too!"

The little ponies and Spike hurried to the Land of Ice and Snow. But Get It and the wizard's snowmen were already there!

"Hand over the Crystal Snowdrop Crown!" said Get It rudely to the Snowflake Princess.

"Little ponies, please help me!" sobbed the princess. "Don't worry! We will!" called Ice Crystal and Tex together.

Ice Crystal made a magic crystal wall to protect the princess and her crown. Tex lassoed Wizard Wantall's snowmen.

Spike breathed out some flames and quickly reduced the snowmen to piles of snow! "That's that!" he laughed.

But Wizard Wantall had been watching and from his magic fountain a big black bird flew out. "Get it!" he ordered.

Before anyone could stop it, the black bird had flown over the ice wall and had seized the Crystal Snowdrop Crown!

"I'll try to lasso it!" cried Tex. "Well done, you've caught it!" cheered Spike. "Oh no, it's fallen onto the wall!"

"My beautiful crown!" wept the princess." It's smashed against the ice and now it's all broken!"

"If you have no crown, Wizard Wantall can come and rule here with his strong magic!" grinned Get It wickedly. "Ha!"

"*Our* magic is just as strong as Wizard Wantall's!" replied Ice Crystal and Snowdrop. "*We* can repair the crown!"

"Crystal snowdrops mend so well, that no one any joins can tell!" And the crown was as good as new again!

So Get It failed again, thanks to the clever little ponies. Do you think Wizard Wantall will ***ever*** *succeed in getting anything he wants?*

HIGHDAYS AND HOLIDAYS IN PONY LAND

WINTER

DECEMBER

All the little ponies look forward to the day in early December when the Christmas Giant comes with his huge sleigh to take them to the Pixie Market, which is held in the Land of Christmas.

They can buy lots of lovely Christmas gifts from stallholders like Yewi the toymaker, Dame Knitting Needles and Merry Marzipan.

JANUARY

In January, the ponies go to the apple orchard where the Apple Goblin lives in an old apple tree. They tie ribbons around the tree and 'Sing the Apples'.

This means they sing a special apple song to the Apple Goblin who then promises the ponies a bumper apple harvest.

FEBRUARY

In February, when there is lots of ice and snow about, Giant Greatoak brings out his Magnificent Mirror so that the little ponies can pretend they are skating on a large, iced pond, but they do not fear the ice breaking!

LITTLE PONY FRIENDS

The Little Ponies have lots of friends,
There's Junk It, Mend It and String Along,
Betsy Bake-a-lot, and old Magician Muddle
Whose spells seem to always go wrong!

Old Tam the Tinker mends their pots and pans,
And Liam the Leprechaun their shoes.
Each night, the Sandman brings lovely dreams,
And Rob Rabbit tells all their news.

The Weather Witch with her golden wand
Makes the sun shine on special days,
And Spike and the dragons are eager to help
In all kinds of different ways.

"LET'S COUNT IN PICTURES!" SAYS SCHOOLTIME